# All About America

# STAGECOACHES AND RAILROADS

## Sally Senzell Isaacs

KINGFISHER
NEW YORK

9|12
20⁰⁰

**All About America: STAGECOACHES AND RAILROADS**

**KINGFISHER**
LONDON & NEW YORK

Copyright © Bender Richardson White 2012

Published in the United States by Kingfisher,
175 Fifth Ave., New York, NY 10010
Kingfisher is an imprint of Macmillan Children's Books, London.
All rights reserved.

Distributed in the U.S. and Canada by Macmillan,
175 Fifth Ave., New York, NY 10010

Library of Congress Cataloging-in-Publication data has been applied for.

ISBN paperback 978-0-7534-6516-5
ISBN reinforced library binding 978-0-7534-6696-4

Kingfisher books are available for special promotions and premiums. For details contact: Special Markets Department, Macmillan, 175 Fifth Ave., New York, NY 10010.

For more information, please visit www.kingfisherbooks.com

Printed in China
10 9 8 7 6 5 4 3 2 1
1TR/0911/WKT/UNTD/140MA

The All About America series was produced for Kingfisher by Bender Richardson White, Uxbridge, U.K.
**Editor:** Lionel Bender
**Designer:** Ben White
**DTP:** Neil Sutton
**Production:** Kim Richardson
**Consultant:** Richard Jensen, Research Professor of History, Culver Stockton College, Missouri

**Sources of quotations and excerpts**
Page 7, reporter's quote: http://bestfriendofcharleston.org
Page 8, 1860 newspaper quote: *Fayetteville Observer*—Thursday evening, May 17, 1860.
Page 9, Constant family story: www.oregonpioneers.com/constant.htm
Page 11, *Omaha Herald* quote: Fradkin, Philip L. *Stagecoach: Wells Fargo and the American West*. New York: Simon & Schuster Source, 2002, page 40.
Page 14, Wells, Fargo & Co. losses: Fradkin, Philip L. *Stagecoach: Wells Fargo and the American West*. New York: Simon & Schuster Source, 2002, pages 95–96.
Page 18, newspaper report quote: Ambrose, Stephen E. *Nothing Like It in the World*. New York: Simon & Schuster, 2000, page 339.
Pages 22, 24, quotes: Editors of Time-Life Books with text by Keith Wheeler. *The Railroaders*. New York: Time-Life Books, 1973, pages 135, 207.
Page 25, Swedish writer quote: Barton, Arnold H. *The Search for Ancestors: A Swedish-American Family Saga*. Carbondale, IL: Southern Illinois University Press, 1979, page 86.
Page 26, Crazy Horse quote: www.nps.gov/jeff/forteachers/upload/Plains_Indians_TAG_7-12.pdf

## Acknowledgments

The publishers would like to thank the following illustrators for their contribution to this book: Mark Bergin, Terry Gabby, Nick Hewetson, Christian Hook, John James, and Gerald Wood. Map: Neil Sutton. Book cover design: Neal Cobourne.

The publishers thank the following for supplying photos for this book: b = bottom, c = center, l = left, t = top, m = middle
© The Art Archive: pages 10m (Gift of Corliss C. and Audrienne Moseley/Buffalo Bill Historical Center, Cody, Wyoming/1.68); 10bl (Granger Collection); 12tl (Bill Manns) • © The Bridgeman Art Library: Boltin Picture Library, page 5; Collection of the New York Historical Society, U.S.A., page 7tl ; Peter Newark Western Americana/Pictures, cover br, pages 11tl, 11m, 14bl, 15bl, 19tl, 23b; Royal Geographical Society, London, page 21t © istockphoto.com: pages 13mr (rcyoung); 14bl (Duncan Walker) • © Library of Congress: pages 1, 2–3, 30–31, 32 (LC-DIG-npcc-28027) • © TopFoto.co.uk: The Granger Collection/TopFoto, cover bl, bc, pages 1, 4tl, 4ml, 4mr, 5t, 5bl, 6t, 6mr, 7mr, 8tl, 8bm, 9tl, 9mr, 12, 12ml, 13m, 13b, 15m, 16tl, 17bm, 19bl, 19br, 20tl, 20tr, 20bl, 22tl, 22mr, 22b, 22–23, 23tr, 24tl, 24bl, 24–25, 25mr, 26tl, 26m, 27tr, 27br, 28tl, 29tl, 29mr.
Every effort has been made to trace the copyright holders of the images. The publishers apologize for any omissions.

**Note to readers:** The website addresses listed in this book are correct at the time of publishing. However, due to the ever-changing nature of the Internet, website addresses and content can change. Websites can contain links that are unsuitable for children. The publisher cannot be held responsible for changes in website addresses or content or for information obtained through third-party websites. We strongly advise that Internet searches should be supervised by an adult.

# CONTENTS

# Introduction

*Stagecoaches and Railroads* looks at the development and growth of transportation in the United States from the time of the first American Indians up to the modern era. It focuses on the introduction and use of boats, stagecoaches, canals, and railroads. It shows how transportation grew in the East and then spread west across the country. The story is presented as a series of double-page articles, each one looking at a particular topic, including how people used stagecoaches and railroads to carry goods and passengers. It is illustrated with paintings, engravings, and photographs from the time, mixed with artists' impressions of everyday scenes and situations.

# A Nation on the Move

## Rivers, roads, and frontier trails

**People have always needed transportation—a way to travel and to move goods from one place to another. As the nation grew from colonial villages to bustling cities, transportation methods were developed that went farther and faster and were more economic.**

The earliest American Indians walked along footpaths and paddled canoes through rivers. The first settlers from Europe learned much from them. The settlers learned how to make canoes from a wood frame covered in bark. They traced the paths along rivers, over hills and mountains, and through forests.

Like the American Indians, settlers found that traveling on water was faster and safer than walking on land paths. In the late 1700s, settlers and explorers built flatboats to paddle down the Ohio, Mississippi, and other rivers. These boxlike boats were 10 to 20 feet (3 to 6 m) wide and could carry far more than canoes could. When families wanted to move, they loaded their belongings onto flatboats. Farmers used flatboats to take their crops to sell in towns along the river.

▲ Traveling by boat in the colonial days

▼ A mast and sail helped this keelboat move along the river.

▼ A famous western artist, Charles M. Russell, painted *When Mules Wear Diamonds,* showing the use of animals for transportation.

## Heading Downstream

Flatboats could travel only one way—in the direction of the river current. When a family used a flatboat to reach their destination, they took the boat apart and used the wood to build a house.

▼ People used flatboats to carry goods downriver. They used oars to help steer the boat.

## The Roughest Routes

Traders heading west traveled through mountain trails in Montana, Wyoming, and Nevada. They used pack animals such as mules and horses to carry heavy loads of goods and supplies to trade with American Indians. They brought back animal hides and furs to sell in the eastern cities. Some miners headed to California gold mines with pack mules.

4

## America's roads

In the mid-1700s, the majority of Americans lived on farms near the Atlantic Ocean. Most travelers rode horses along narrow paths. Farmers pulled wagons to take their crops to markets. Merchants hauled goods from the seaports to their stores. In the early 1800s, some enterprising individuals built toll roads. They smoothed and widened the dirt paths. Then they put up poles across the road every few miles or so. Travelers had to stop and pay a toll to pass through.

◀ A toy stagecoach

## Stagecoaches

Stagecoaches had been used in England since 1670. They were brought to America in the 1730s. In 1785, the U.S. Congress began a mail service by stagecoach. It was a safer, more reliable way to get mail between cities. On a passenger stagecoach, several people rode together. Each trip was made in stages, stopping to change horses and let passengers off.

## Wagon trains to the West

By 1821, some businessmen wanted to travel west of the Mississippi River. Traders loaded wagons with cloth and other goods to sell in Spanish villages in New Mexico. Miners formed wagon trains to California to join the gold rush, starting in 1848. Families packed what they could fit into their wagons and headed west to build new homes in Oregon and California. People traveled together in wagon trains along well-known trails, such as the Sante Fe and Oregon trails.

▼ A wagon train on the Sante Fe Trail. The trail went from Franklin, Missouri, to Santa Fe, New Mexico.

## BOSTON, Plymouth & Sandwich MAIL STAGE,

*CONTINUES TO RUN AS FOLLOWS:*

LEAVES Boston every Tuesday, Thursday, and Saturday mornings at 5 o'clock, breakfast at Leonard's, Scituate; dine at Bradford's, Plymouth; and arrive in Sandwich the same evening. Leaves Sandwich every Monday, Wednesday and Friday mornings; breakfast at Bradford's, Plymouth; dine at Leonard's, Scituate, and arrive in Boston the same evening.

Passing through Dorchester, Quincy, Wyemouth, Hingham, Scituate, Hanover, Pembroke, Duxbury, Kingston, Plymouth to Sandwich. *Fare,* from Boston to Scituate, 1 doll. 25 cts. From Boston to Plymouth, 2 dolls. 50 cts. From Boston to Sandwich, 3 dolls. 63 cts.

N. B. Extra Carriages can be obtained of the proprietor's, at Boston and Plymouth, at short notice. STAGE BOOKS kept at Boyden's Market-square, Boston.

# The First Locomotives
## The power of steam turns wheels

For a horse, it was easier to pull a wagon on iron wheels rolling on iron rails than it was to pull a stagecoach. Why? Because the wheels rolled very freely. The invention of the steam engine made possible a locomotive that pulled the wagons.

Steam-powered trains started to replace horse-drawn trains in 1804. A British engineer, Richard Trevithick, built the first train steam engine, or locomotive. Trevithick's first locomotive hauled five wagons of iron ore and 70 passengers. It traveled for 9 miles (14.5 km) at a speed of 5 miles (8 km) per hour. British and American inventors soon built faster and stronger locomotives. One of the first Americans to build a locomotive was Peter Cooper. He named his train *Tom Thumb* because of its small size.

### Tom Thumb's Race
Is a steam engine faster than a horse? With cheering passengers on his small train, Peter Cooper drove *Tom Thumb* in a race against a horse-drawn train in 1830. The locomotive looked like a sure win, but then something snapped on the engine. The horse won this famous race.

► The *Stourbridge Lion* was made in England and delivered to the town of Honesdale, Pennsylvania, in 1829.

This locomotive ran in Mississippi around 1836.

### How Steam Works
Locomotives had engines that combined fire and water to make steam. Workers made fires by shoveling wood or coal into the engine's firebox. The heat traveled in metal pipes to a boiler filled with water. As the water boiled from the heat, it made steam. The steam created pressure that, through pistons and rods, moved the train's wheels.

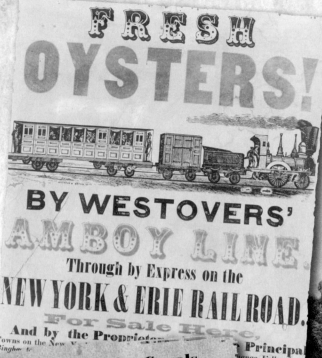

FRESH OYSTERS!

BY WESTOVERS'

AMBOY LINE.

Through by Express on the

NEW YORK & ERIE RAIL ROAD.

For Sale Here,

And by the Proprietors

Towns on the New Y...

Binghamton...

...Principal

...ango Valley, from

...ll be sup-

...best of AMBOY

...OVER.

## The fastest way to travel

The *Best Friend of Charleston* was America's first regular passenger train service. It made its first 6-mile (10-km) run in Charleston, South Carolina, on December 25, 1830. A reporter for the *Charleston Courier* wrote: "The 141 persons flew on the wings of wind at a speed of 15 to 24 miles per hour, annihilating time and space . . . leaving all the world behind." Six months later, the train met a tragic end when a crewman wrongly closed a safety valve on the engine and the locomotive exploded.

▼ The Erie Canal at Lockport, New York, in 1838

### Pulled along Canals

Animals powered the canal boats. Horses or mules walked on a path beside the canal, attached to the boat by ropes. At locks, the animals were unhitched, the water level and boats raised or lowered, and the animals rehitched. In 1850, canal boats carried most of the nation's freight between cities.

## Traveling on canals

Many states were busy digging canals, which are waterways that connect rivers and lakes. New York's Erie Canal was the longest canal by far. Completed in 1825, it ran 363 miles (584 km), from Lake Erie to the Hudson River, which flows to the Atlantic Ocean. A canal ride along its length took eight days. That was a big improvement over the 20-day trip on the roads. Cities by the canals, such as Cleveland, Ohio, doubled in population as trade grew.

▲ By 1869, railroads crossed the eastern United States and the transcontinental railroad reached California.

# West by Steam Power
## Steamboats on the rivers

By 1820, the nation was spreading west. People from eastern cities moved to farmland in Kentucky, Illinois, and Indiana. They needed better ways to transport their crops to cities in the East and to ports by the oceans.

▲ John Fitch's steamboat

### America's First
John Fitch built the first successful steamboat in the United States. He sailed it on the Delaware River in 1787. Watching the event were members of the Constitutional Convention, who were drawing up plans for the first U.S. government.

Since the nation had few railroads, the steamboat was their answer. Unlike flatboats that could only follow river currents, steam-powered boats could travel in any direction. By the 1830s, steamboats, with their big paddle wheels and tall smokestacks, floated up and down the rivers. Heading to the western frontier, the boats carried animals, tools, and furniture on the lower decks. On the upper decks, passengers traveled comfortably. An 1860 newspaper described a steamboat in North Carolina called the *A.P. Hurt*: "There are six state-rooms [for sleeping] . . . a saloon and dining apartment, a social hall . . . where gentlemen may smoke . . . a room, the last aft, for ladies traveling with children. All these are fitted up in good taste and excellent style."

▼ In the 1830s, Cherokee Indians being taken to Indian Territory traveled across the Mississippi by steamboats.

### "Steamboat's Comin'!"
With its puffing chimneys and well-known whistle, the steamboat pulled up to its landings beside southern cotton plantations. Slaves hauled bales of cotton onto the boat. Then the boat headed down the Mississippi River to New Orleans. The cotton was sold there and shipped to cloth mills in Europe or eastern U.S. cities.

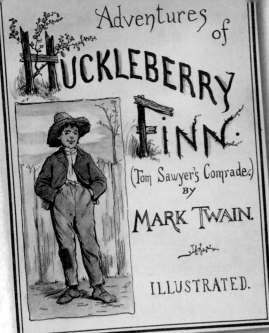

*Adventures of* HUCKLEBERRY FINN.

(Tom Sawyer's Comrade.)

BY

MARK TWAIN.

ILLUSTRATED.

*Mark Twain*

◀ An original edition from 1885 of *Adventures of Huckleberry Finn* by Mark Twain

## Transportation to the West

In the 1850s, people could travel north and south most easily by steamboat and east and west by railroad. Neither trains nor steamboats went much farther than the Mississippi River. For the 300,000 to 500,000 pioneers who kept moving west to Oregon Territory and California, there were wagon trails to travel on.

Pioneers Lavina and Isaac Constant and their five children started their journey west in March 1852. First they traveled by train from their hometown of Springfield, Illinois, to St. Louis, Missouri. Then they rode a steamboat to Independence, Missouri. They brought their wagon, horses, and mules on the boat. At Independence, the Constants joined 25 other covered wagons in a wagon train on the Oregon Trail. Their trip to Oregon took five months.

### Mark Twain

When Samuel Clemens wrote stories, he used the pen name Mark Twain. He grew up in Hannibal, Missouri, next to the Mississippi River. He watched steamboats on the river and learned to be a steamboat pilot. He also became a writer, and his famous characters Huckleberry Finn and Tom Sawyer had river adventures of their own.

▶ A color wood engraving from 1884 of a train in Rahway, New Jersey

HOTEL

### Railroads vs. Steamboats

The first railroad bridge over the Mississippi River was built in 1856. Steamboat owners tried to stop it. They said it would be a danger to steamboats. They also probably feared losing business to the railroads. Two weeks after the bridge opened, a steamboat hit the bridge. A fire broke out that destroyed the boat and bridge.

▶ By the 1850s, trains like this one stopped at cloth mills in New Hampshire and Massachusetts to deliver cotton and pick up finished cloth.

# Stagecoaches Out West
## Delivering passengers, mail, money, and gold

In 1847, California belonged to Mexico. The following year, it was part of the United States and gold was discovered in a river near San Francisco. Hundreds of thousands of people headed for California. To transport them, a stagecoach business was started.

◀ **California miners sifted dirt from streams to find gold.**

Not only gold miners headed to California in 1848. Others moved there to start new businesses such as clothing stores, hotels, and banks. All of these new people needed a safe and fast means of transportation. They needed a way to get into and out of town. They needed to send home letters and money and to receive supplies, newspapers, and mail.

In 1852, a New York business called Wells, Fargo & Company opened its first office in San Francisco and 12 other offices in towns near the mines. As a bank and stagecoach company, Wells Fargo promised a safe and fast way to transport mail, passengers, packages, money, and gold.

### Crossing the Nation
Travel time from New York to California varied greatly:
- Sailing ship from New York to Panama; then a mule trek or walk across the Isthmus of Panama; then another ship to California: 3–5 months
- Sailing ship around the tip of South America and up the Pacific coast: 5–12 months
- Overland wagon train that stopped each night: 6–12 months

▶ **Stagecoaches ran 24 hours a day through scorching deserts and rough mountain passes.**

▼ **A Wells Fargo stagecoach**

WELLS FARGO & CO. OVERLAND STAGE.
US MAIL.

### A Stagecoach Ride
One popular stagecoach model had nine seats. Three people faced forward, three faced backward, and three sat in the middle with a choice of which way to face. Luggage and mail rode on the top, sometimes with an extra passenger or two. On long journeys, passengers slept uncomfortably in their seats.

# Long and uncomfortable journeys

Much of the stagecoach travel ran between western towns. However, some people traveled by stagecoach 3,000 miles (4,800 km) across the country. About every 12 miles (20 km), the stagecoach stopped at a station. At "swing stations," the driver changed horses or mules. At "home stations," a family cooked meals and provided a bed for the driver to take a nap.

Along the way, surprises popped up in the form of thunderstorms, flooded rivers, and robbers. A writer for the *Omaha Herald* in Nebraska warned stagecoach travelers: "Don't imagine for a moment you are going on a picnic; expect annoyances; discomfort and some hardships. If you are disappointed, thank heaven."

◀ A Wells, Fargo & Co. mailbox

▼ Stagecoaches stopped at offices to pick up mail and money.

## A Trusty Mail Service

In the mid-1880s, the U.S. government delivered mail, but it was overwhelmed by all the mail going west. Wells Fargo speedily set up its offices in drugstores and general stores. People trusted Wells Fargo to send their mail safely.

## A Stagecoach Network

By 1866, stagecoaches served mining towns in Colorado, Montana, Nevada, Utah, and Idaho. Wells, Fargo & Co. bought up other stagecoach companies to own the largest stagecoach network in the world.

# The Pony Express

## A successful but doomed postal service

As western towns grew, some stagecoach owners wondered, What's a faster way to get the mail across the plains, deserts, and mountains to the West? Their answer was the Pony Express.

A Pony Express rider's saddle with locked pockets for the mail

Running pony logo used by the early U.S. postal service

Stagecoaches delivered mail from Missouri to California in 18 to 24 days. In 1860, William Russell, Alexander Majors, and William Waddell promised to cut the delivery time to ten days. For their Pony Express service, they hired 80 young riders and bought 400 horses. They set up 190 stations about 10 miles (16 km) apart.

On April 3, 1860, the first Pony Express rider waited at the train station in St. Joseph, Missouri. The train pulled in, and a worker handed a bundle of mail to the rider. The rider galloped to the next station, where a fresh horse awaited him. At about every third station, the rider stopped to rest. After about 100 miles (160 km), he handed the mail to the next rider, who sped off toward Kansas, Nebraska, Wyoming, Utah, and Nevada. On April 13, the mail reached Sacramento, California.

These stamps show that this letter was handled by the U.S. Post Office and the Pony Express.

◀ Paiute Indians sometimes chased Pony Express riders off their homeland.

### A Dangerous Ride

The Pony Express route in Nevada and Utah ran right over the hunting and burial grounds of the Paiute Indians. In the summer of 1860, the Paiute attacked Pony Express riders and stations. They killed horses and riders and destroyed seven stations.

## The Pony Express has a short life

The relay system succeeded in delivering the mail in the fastest way possible. However, it stopped after 19 months of service. There were two reasons for its demise. First, the business ran at a loss. The cost of stations, horses, and workers was much greater than the money brought in. Second, the telegraph service reached the West.

## Technology beats horsepower

Since 1844, people in the East had been using the telegraph to send important messages. Reporters sent news stories by telegraph. Train conductors sent messages to stations about delays. Telegraph messages traveled through electrical wires that were strung between poles. An operator clicked out electrical signals in a code of dots and dashes. At another location, an operator received the coded message and translated it into words. By October 1861, telegraph lines and offices had reached most western towns. People no longer needed the Pony Express.

▼ A Pony Express station at the head of Echo Canyon in Utah

### Sending Messages

When people wanted to send telegraph messages, they went to a telegraph office. Many offices were in train stations. A person told the message to an operator, who tapped the coded words into the telegraph machine. The person paid for each word of the message.

## Technology Catches Up

Telegraph workers set up their poles along railroad tracks and well-known trails. Pony Express riders passed them, sometimes shouting messages from other workers up the trail. On October 24, 1861, the president of the Overland Telegraph Company sent one of the first transcontinental telegrams. It was sent from San Francisco to President Abraham Lincoln in Washington, D.C.

▲ A telegraph machine (not wired up). The messages were known as telegrams, and the signals were called Morse code, after their U.S. inventor, Samuel Morse. At the receiving end, each message was written down and sent to its destination.

# "It's a Holdup!"

## Stagecoach bandits—armed robbers

Passengers boarded a stagecoach in a bustling town. But soon the coach bumped along silent, empty roads. That's where bandits hid. As the coach approached, the bandits pounced from behind trees.

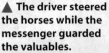

Hungry for a stagecoach's gold, silver, and money, bandits waited in places where the horses had to slow down, such as at a sharp bend or a steep slope. Then they pounced, shouting, "Halt! Throw down the box!" The bandits carried rifles and guns. So did the stagecoach company's messenger, who sat beside the driver as a guard. Some passengers also carried guns. But when bandits struck, fearful passengers usually tossed out their money and jewelry, and the messenger handed over the treasure box to protect the passengers.

▲ The driver steered the horses while the messenger guarded the valuables.

▲ A mix of rifles and guns used by stagecoach company staff

## The cost of trouble

Stagecoach robberies started in 1856, and the last one was in 1916. Wells, Fargo & Company reported 313 stagecoach robberies from 1870 to 1884. In total, four passengers, four stage drivers, two guards, and five robbers had lost their lives. The cost of those robberies was $928,000 (worth $16 million today). This included $415,000 in stolen metal and money, plus reward money and the paychecks for guards, attorneys, and officers.

▼ Two Wells, Fargo & Co. messengers sit for a photo with their rifles.

### Armed Guards

On the coach, valuables traveled in a large locked box under the driver's feet. The messenger sat beside the driver and waited for trouble. His main job was to protect the box. The stagecoach company paid the messenger well and armed him with a sawed-off, double-barreled shotgun or a breech-loading rifle. At the first sign of bandits, the messenger would draw his weapon and try to frighten them off by firing a few shots above their heads.

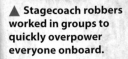

▲ Stagecoach robbers worked in groups to quickly overpower everyone onboard.

## Unexpected problems

Besides facing robberies, passengers occasionally had to jump down and push the coach out of the mud. Sometimes they had to stay for days at a station because a river was flooded or a wheel was broken. Inside the coach, space was limited. If the driver threw in an extra bag of mail, passengers had to crowd close together. A popular list of travelers' tips warned passengers not to "lop over neighbors when sleeping."

$250 REWARD!

A REWARD OF $250 WILL be paid by Wells, Fargo & Co. for the arrest and conviction of each of the parties who attempted to rob our TREASURE BOX,

Will on the night of Oct. 19th,

▲ Bandit Charles Bolton called himself Black Bart. People said he waved his gun at holdups but he never used it.

◄ A Wells, Fargo & Co. sign offering a reward for catching stagecoach robbers

## Big Bad Bart
Charles Bolton held up 28 stagecoaches. He always left a poem at the scene, signed "Black Bart, the po8" (poet). At his last holdup, he also accidentally left his handkerchief that had a symbol from his laundry. Lawmen went to the laundry, found his address, and arrested him.

15

# Masses on the Move
## Railroads boosted by national conflict

From 1861 to 1865, the United States was a divided nation. During the Civil War, many battles raged, causing chaos to transportation. Because railroads played a big part in the North's victory, their development was boosted after the war.

War broke out in April 1861, and soldiers signed up to fight for their sides. Southern states wanted to start their own nation and allow people to own slaves. Northern states wanted to keep the nation together and stop slavery from spreading. By the time the war had ended, more than 600,000 soldiers had died.

Civil War battles took place mainly in the Southeast. Most of the nation's railroad lines and factories were in the northern states. Trains moved soldiers to battlefields, along with their cannons, horses, food, tents, and other supplies.

▲ At the end of the Civil War, the North's General William T. Sherman commanded his troops to tear up tracks in Georgia and leave the South in shambles.

▶ Tracks were laid through rugged western mountains. Surveyors measured and plotted the railroad routes.

▼ The northern army set up huge railroad supply centers.

### Railroads as Vital Links
As the North and South fought, there was talk of linking the East and West by railroad. By 1861, there were already thousands of miles of railroad tracks east of the Mississippi River. The following year, work started on connecting those railroads to towns in California and Oregon so masses of pioneers could move west.

## The war delays progress

While railroad companies wanted to lay tracks across the continent, the Civil War made it difficult for them. In 1862, President Abraham Lincoln signed the Pacific Railway Act. It handed over the building of tracks to the Union Pacific Railroad Company, starting in the East, and the Central Pacific Company, starting in the West. Congress gave each company $16,000 ($360,000 at today's value) for each mile (1.6 km) of track it built across the plains and $48,000 ($1.1 million) for each mile in high mountain areas. But with many men at war, there were too few workers to lay tracks.

### Central Pacific Railroad

Starting in Sacramento, California, the company needed thousands of workers to build 689 miles (1,109 km) of track. Charles Crocker sent agents to China to advertise railroad jobs. He also recruited in San Francisco's Chinatown, where men had left the empty gold mines. Around 12,000 Chinese workers helped build the transcontinental railroad.

### Union Pacific Railroad

Union Pacific built tracks that headed westward from Omaha, Nebraska. After the Civil War, thousands of soldiers became railroad workers. Newly freed slaves took railroad jobs, too. Immigrants arrived from Ireland and Germany and headed to the construction sites. They were happy to finally have work. Union Pacific workers laid 1,086 miles (1,748 km) of tracks.

▼ In 1867, an artist engraved this picture of Union Pacific workers.

### A time of change

In 1865, the South surrendered the war. Soldiers returned home, and the nation turned its attention to the transcontinental railroad. It would bring many changes. People would be able to move to the open land in the middle of the country. There they could build farms, towns, and ranches. Life would also change for the American Indians who lived there. Railroads, farms, and towns would force them off their land forever.

17

# Linking the Continent
## America's greatest construction project

Blizzards buried rail crews in the mountains. American Indians attacked them on the plains. Flooding rivers washed away the previous day's construction. As workers teetered on high bridges, this project seemed doomed!

▲ A locomotive with steam up and ready to roll

▼ Workers balance themselves, as on a tightrope, while they hoist up the wood to build this trestle bridge.

Starting in the flatlands of Nebraska, Union Pacific proudly laid 6 miles (10 km) of track a day. For a while, its biggest challenge was getting lumber for the rails. With no trees on the plains, the company sent lumber on boats up the Missouri River and then hauled it to the workers by horse and wagon. In the winter, workers built temporary railroad tracks on the frozen river and sent their supplies by train. Once the crew got to Wyoming, they hit the challenge of blasting tunnels through the Rocky Mountains.

Meanwhile, the Central Pacific crew tried to blast its way through the granite cliffs of the Sierra Nevada. Day after day, workers dragged blasting powder and tools to the mountain cliffs. They blasted, drilled, and dug. The Central Pacific made 15 tunnels. The Union Pacific made four tunnels.

### Building Bridges
To build tracks over rivers and streams, crews bolted together wooden trestle bridges. One newspaper reported that such bridges would "shake the nerves of the stoutest hearts when they see . . . [what is] expected to uphold a train in motion." Some of the trestle bridges could not take the weight of a train and collapsed, causing death and injury to many passengers and crew members.

Union Pacific's poster advertising a ride on the first transcontinental railroad

An 1860s locomotive

## The Final Spike

As the crowd cheered, railroad officials drove in special silver and gold spikes given by various states. Then California's governor, Leland Stanford, took a silver hammer and drove in the last golden spike. Two engines chugged toward each other. They stopped, and their engineers got out to shake hands.

The Golden Spike ceremony at Promontory Summit, Utah, on May 10, 1869

## A race to the end

Newspaper reports called it the "greatest railroad construction race in the history of the world." When the Union Pacific crew laid 6 miles (10 km) of track, the Central Pacific speeded up to lay 7 miles (11 km). Finally the heads of the two companies bet $10,000 that they would be the first to lay 10 miles (16 km) in one day. Like a fine-tuned machine, the Central Pacific crew hauled 3,520 rails, 25,800 ties, and 55,000 spikes. After 12 hours, they laid 10 miles of track! It was a world record.

Twelve days later, on May 10, 1869, the two crews met at Promontory Summit, Utah, and the tracks were completed. Telegraph operators tapped out the word "Done!" The nation celebrated, including ringing the Liberty Bell in Philadelphia.

The "Last Spike" is now in a museum at Stanford University in California. The ceremony was planned for May 8, but it was postponed. The date on the spike could not be changed.

The Pacific Railroad ground broken Jany 8th 1863 and completed May 8th 1869

19

# Railroad Towns
## Trains deliver many changes

Soon after the Promontory Summit celebration, railroad companies built four more transcontinental railroads. Towns sprang up wherever railroad lines crossed.

The owners of railroads encouraged people to move to railroad towns. More citizens in a town meant more money for the railroad companies that owned the land. Every railroad town had houses, stores, banks, restaurants, and hotels. Railroad owners brought in new residents by selling them land cheaply. Some gave away seeds and farm equipment to get people started.

The owners of the railroad companies became rich. Many people accused them of being greedy. For example, the wealthy William H. Vanderbilt bought up many small railroad companies. He fought against government laws that would control the railroads. Big companies like his agreed on prices and put small companies out of business.

▲ The Great Railroad Strike of 1877 started in West Virginia and spread to New York.

▲ An 1879 cartoon criticizing William H. Vanderbilt (top) and other railroad owners. Vanderbilt was one of the richest men in the world.

▼ A poster from 1882 advertising the route for the Illinois Central Railroad (I.C.R.R.)

## Strikes and Violence

By 1877, many railroad companies had expanded so much that they were running out of money. They cut their workers' paychecks but continued to pay dividends to their investors. When the B&O Railroad cut wages, its crews went on strike, or stopped working. The trains could not run without their workers. State governors sent troops to force the workers back. Violence broke out in the streets, and people were injured.

▲ A railroad town as the train arrives

## The frontier opens

A frontier is the land between the settled part of the country and the wilderness. In the 1890s, railroads crisscrossed the frontier land of Kansas, Nebraska, the Dakotas, Colorado, and Wyoming. Railroad companies sold land cheaply, and the government offered free land to anyone who would build a home, farm, or ranch on it. Pioneers left city life and took a chance on the frontier. They wanted to live near railroad towns. Farmers and ranchers brought their cattle and crops to the trains. They shopped at the stores in the towns.

Frontier people did not feel connected to rules and laws from the East. Western towns had a marshal who tried to keep order. Sometimes cowboys went through towns as they led cattle from ranches to the railroads. They could get loud and rowdy. These were the Wild West days now made famous in movies.

### Railroad Land

The U.S. government helped railroad companies build the nation's tracks. Congress gave the companies millions of acres of free land. The companies built their railroad tracks and sold the surrounding land to settlers through land grant offices. The settlers then lived in tents until they built their houses.

### Connecting Communities

Because of the railroads, quiet towns such as Salt Lake City, Utah, and Denver, Colorado, became big cities. An arriving train brought the day's biggest excitement. Some passengers left the train and boarded a stagecoach to visit friends or family nearby. Ongoing passengers got off to eat a quick meal before riding off again. Trains arrived and left every day.

# Traveling in Style
## Mr. Pullman's luxury trains

*"The six months' journey is reduced to less than a week. The prairie schooner [covered wagon] has passed away, and is replaced by the railway coach with all its modern comforts."*

▲ A railroad conductor's pocket watch case

### Pullman Car

From the first time he tried to sleep on an uncomfortable train, George Pullman started designing dining cars and sleeping cars that became famous around the world. His first designs had tables and beds fitted with hinges. When they were not in use, they were folded flat on the wall.

The statement above appeared on December 11, 1869, in *Frank Leslie's Illustrated Newspaper*. Trains offered a faster, cheaper service than any other means of transportation. In 1865, it took months to travel by steamboat and wagon train from New York to California at a cost of more than $1,000 (worth $13,800 today). After 1869, transcontinental trains made the trip in seven days.

The most expensive transcontinental train trip was $150 ($2,480 today). But if people were willing to sit on a stiff bench for a week, they could travel for $65 ($1,070 today). They might have luggage piled around their feet or fellow passengers asleep on their shoulders, but they were traveling with a roof over their heads. Meanwhile, in the first-class train cars, passengers slept in beds with fresh sheets.

▼ A Pullman dining car

▶ The railroad staff made the beds for the passengers.

## Train Wrecks

Most trains arrived safely, but accidents sometimes happened. Bridges and tunnels collapsed. Trains collided. Connecting pins between cars fell out and sent runaway trains down the tracks. In 1887, the Bussey Bridge collapsed in Massachusetts. Thirty-seven people died, and many others were injured.

◀ An 1876 engraving of a Pullman parlor car on the Pennsylvania Railroad

▲ The Bussey Bridge collapse and train wreck, March 14, 1887

## A vacation on wheels

Wealthy people bought special tickets that allowed them to use any Pullman car on a train. A Pullman dining car was as fancy as the nation's best restaurants. Passengers sat at tables while waiters served such extravagant food as oyster soup and antelope steaks. Pullman sleeping cars had fold-down beds and hot-air furnaces. Some also had a library, a hair salon, and a drawing-room or parlor area where passengers sat on soft sofas while the conductor played organ music.

On a long railroad journey, the view out the window changed every day. Some days brought vast plains. Others brought pine forests, majestic mountain peaks, and deserts. And all in great comfort.

## Eating on the Run

The first railcars resembled stagecoaches on wheels. Later, first- and second-class cars were made. Before dining cars, trains stopped at stations for 10 minutes to let passengers eat at a platform restaurant. Passengers paid for their meals before they ate. When the train whistle blew, everyone ran out the door and boarded the train.

▲ An 1880 advertisement showing a restaurant at a train stop

# Advertising for Immigrants
## Starting a new life in the West

Railroad companies wanted to sell their western land. Thanks to their great advertising, they attracted thousands of people from all over the world to move to the West in the late 1800s.

Much of the land owned by the railroads suffered from winter blizzards, grasshopper attacks, and prairie fires set by the local American Indians. None of this was mentioned in the railroad company advertisements. They sent out "Land for Sale" ads, in ten different languages, all over the world.

From 1850 to 1900, millions of people left their homes in Europe and traveled by steamships to America. People left countries such as Germany, Ireland, and Sweden because of unemployment and lack of good farmland and to escape punishment for their religious beliefs. When these immigrants arrived in the United States, many stayed in eastern cities and worked in factories. Others wanted to own land and farms. They boarded trains to the West.

▲ An 1882 poster wishing good luck to westward travelers

▼ A poster from the 1870s offering free homestead land for a train ticket west

**2,000,000** FARMS of Fertile Prairie Lands to be had Free of Cost

**CENTRAL DAKOTA**

**30 Millions OF Acres**

**YOU NEED A FARM!**

**CHICAGO AND NORTHWESTERN**

**HOW TO GET THERE**

## You Need a Farm!

Railroad companies posted signs in crowded cities. Some offered free farms. One sign from the Great Northern Railway asked, "Are you tired of working for others? Is the daily grind of office or factory beginning to get on your nerves? . . . Why not go where you can make a good living at pleasant and profitable work . . . Go west—buy five or ten acres of Washington Fruit Land."

▼ The train dropped off immigrant families near their new farmland.

Free Lands
And Dry Farming In The Southwest

Santa Fe

RANCHO DEL PASO
RANCH OF THE PASS

SACRAMENTO, CAL.
SACRAMENTO VALLEY
COLONIZATION CO.

FREE LANDS
IN THE
Shoshone Reservation
OF
Wyoming

Burlington Route

A Synopsis
of the
Homestead and
Desert Land Laws
of the
United States

▲ These railroad brochures
helped sell land to immigrants.

## Wooing the Russians

A large group of Mennonites from Russia decided to become farmers in Kansas. First their train stopped in Nebraska, where clever land agents tried to encourage them to stay. They pretended that the Russians' luggage was lost. Meanwhile, they showed them their beautiful farmland and offered free hay and windmills if they stayed. The Russians decided to continue on to Kansas.

▲ Passengers with less
expensive train tickets rode
in cars like this on the
Northern Pacific Railroad.

## Building communities

Some railroad agents went to Europe, put together up to 100 immigrant families, and brought them to Iowa, Kansas, or Nebraska to start their own communities. There they could speak their own language and share the same customs. The railroad company offered them cheap tickets on ships and trains and sold them cheap land. If these immigrants liked their new home, they would write to their friends and relatives to join them. Then the railroads could ship lumber to build more houses and coal to heat them.

A Swedish writer told how his family felt in their home beside a railroad: the "house was so drafty that you could smell the coal smoke inside when trains would pass on the Chicago and Northwestern track . . ."

# Chasing Land and Loot
## The "iron horse" pushes out American Indians

Long before the arrival of trains, stagecoaches, or any white settlers, more than five million American Indians lived in the present-day United States. By 1890, only 250,000 remained. The tribes on the Great Plains survived until the railroads changed their lives.

Crazy Horse, a Sioux leader in 1874, said, "The Great Spirit gave us plenty of land to live on, and buffalo, deer, antelope, and other game. But you have come here; you are taking my land from me; you are killing off our game, so it is hard for us to live." By the 1860s, the U.S. government wanted to settle the entire continent. Its leaders made treaties with the Great Plains tribes. They promised to move the tribes to reservations where they could live alone peacefully. Some of the promises were broken.

▲ An engraving of an American Indian ceremony to bring back the buffalo

▶ A 1910 painting by Charles M. Russell called *Trail of the Iron Horse*. "Iron horse" was a term many writers and artists used for a locomotive.

## Living with Buffalo
Great Plains tribes included the Sioux, Pawnee, and Cheyenne. They lived in portable tepees and moved often to follow the buffalo herds. Buffalo meat was their food. Buffalo skins provided clothes, blankets, shoes, and tepees. They used the horns for cups and bowls, and the ribs served as snow sleds.

## Destroying the Buffalo
Around 1850, there were more than six million buffalo on the Great Plains. As white settlers built their towns, the animals starved or were frightened away. Railroad construction was the final blow. Hunters killed millions of buffalo. The meat fed the railroad crews, and the hides were taken by trains to markets in the East. Hunting parties sometimes shot buffalo from trains.

A train robbery scene on a poster for Buffalo Bill Cody's tent show

▶ A "wanted" poster for Bill Doolin issued after he and his gang held up a train in Oklahoma in May 1895

$5,000.00
REWARD
FOR CAPTURE
DEAD OR ALIVE
OF
BILL DOOLIN
NOTORIOUS ROBBER OF
TRAINS AND BANKS
ABOUT 6 FOOT 2 INCHES TALL, LT. BROWN HAIR,
DANGEROUS, ALWAYS HEAVILY ARMED.

## It's an attack!

Some American Indians went peacefully to reservations in the Dakotas and Wyoming. The U.S. Army forced others off their lands. Some American Indians went after the railroads for ruining their lives. Sometimes they removed spikes from the tracks and bent the rails. Locomotives flipped off the tracks, causing horrible damage and death to passengers on that train and any others that crashed into it.

## Train robbers

Wild West gangs attacked trains, too. They wanted to steal money and valuables. Sometimes a couple of gang members boarded a train like passengers. They overtook the driver and stopped the train. The rest of the gang jumped aboard, robbed the passengers, and dynamited the train's safe. Wild West gangs were always hiding out from sheriffs and U.S. marshals.

### The Wild Bunch

Bill Doolin called his gang the Wild Bunch. In 1874, two teenage girls joined the gang. They were Annie McDougal (called Cattle Annie) and Jennie Metcalf (called Little Britches). The girls served as lookouts. They fired warning shots when anyone approached the gang's hideout. Both girls were sharpshooters, but they eventually got caught and went to prison.

▶ Cattle Annie and Little Britches

# Back on Track

## Railroads after the frontier days

For more than 100 years, railroads were the most popular way to travel across the United States. Then, in the 1940s, a new invention, the automobile, took over. But the trains of the old West live on through books, songs, and movies.

Throughout the late 1800s and early 1900s, most people rode a train at some time, and trains captured the imagination of almost everyone. Trains stood for adventure. Writers wrote plays, books, movies, and songs about trains. People everywhere read "dime novels" (short stories that usually cost 10¢) about iron horses and train bandits in the Wild West.

In 1896, Scott Marble wrote a play called *The Great Train Robbery*. When the inventor Thomas Edison saw the play, he decided to make a movie based on the story. This was the first western movie. It was hailed as America's first great box-office hit. In 1903, the first crowd to see it in New York City cheered for so long that the theater played it again three more times.

◄ A 1913 painting called *The Engineer*

### Railroad Hero

One of the most famous songs about the early railroads is "The Ballad of Casey Jones." Jones was a railroad engineer who became the hero in an accident on April 30, 1900. He tried to stop a passenger train he was driving, the "Cannonball Special," from colliding with a broken-down freight train. The trains did collide and he was killed, but his action of braking hard and blowing the train whistle saved the passengers.

### When I Grow Up . . .

In the 1900s, many children dreamed of growing up to be a railroad engineer. Toy and model train collecting and keeping scrapbooks of locomotive illustrations as hobbies kept them happy.

▲ A painting of a high-speed steam locomotive from 1937

◄ A poster for a new railroad service, 1942

## Transportation changes

Trains changed the nation forever. They connected towns and cities all across the continent. People could travel freely for work, to visit family, and for vacations.

By the 1920s, most American families owned a car. Instead of following train schedules, people preferred to drive whenever they wished and in the privacy of their own vehicles. In the 1940s, the U.S. government built highways instead of railroad tracks. Buses and trucks carried the passengers and goods that once traveled on trains. By the 1950s, people flew on jet planes.

In recent years, passenger trains have been getting attention again. They use less energy and create less pollution than cars and planes, and they move many people at once without creating traffic on the roads. It looks as though train transportation is here to stay!

The New EMPIRE STATE EXPRESS
NEW YORK CENTRAL SYSTEM

▼ A 1915 advertisement for a Wells, Fargo & Co. train service

### Commuter Trains

As cities grew, people began to ride trains to their work from their homes in the suburbs. In cities such as New York, some tracks run underground and others are elevated above the streets. In the suburbs, tracks are at street level.

ACROSS THE CONTINENT

Once 32 days Now 4 days

THE FARGO WAY

### Chugging into the Future

In 1925, the first diesel electric locomotive in the United States started replacing the steam engine. It could reach speeds of 100 miles (160 km) per hour. In 2000, a fully electric train service started between Boston and Washington, D.C., that travels at speeds of up to 150 miles (240 km) per hour. It is known as a high-speed rail service.

# Glossary

**bandit** a robber who carries a gun and is usually part of a gang

**canal** a manmade water highway

**Civil War (1861–1865)** in the United States, a war over slavery between the northern and southern states

**conductor** a person who collects the tickets and is in charge of a train

**Congress** the branch of U.S. government that makes laws

**engineer** a person who runs a locomotive

**freight** goods that are transported

**frontier** the land between the settled part of a country and the wilderness

**general store** a place that sells many different things, such as food and tools

**gold rush** starting in 1848, the time when many people gave up their ordinary lives and went to California to find gold

**immigrant** someone who arrives from another country and settles

**investor** a person who puts money into a business and expects to make a lot more money in return

**Isthmus of Panama** the narrow strip of land that separates the Atlantic and Pacific oceans and connects North and South America

**locomotive** an engine used to pull a train

**lumber** wood that has been sawed and will be used for building

**marshal** a law officer of a town

**mill** a building with machines for grinding grain or making cloth

**plains** a wide area of flat or gently rolling land. The Great Plains lie between the Mississippi River and the Rockies.

**plantation** a large farm for cotton and other crops

**rail** a length of iron or steel laid across railroad ties to make tracks

**ranch** a farm where cattle, horses, or sheep are raised

**reservation** an area of land set aside for American Indians to live on

**settler** a person who makes a home in a new place

**sheriff** an officer who tries to keep order in a county

**slave** someone who is owned by another person and is made to work for that person

**spike** a large, strong nail

**stagecoach** a boxlike car pulled by horses in which people traveled long distances

**surveyor** a person who looks at and measures land for setting boundaries or building something such as a railroad

**telegraph** a machine that sent messages in code through electrical wires

**tepee** a cone-shaped tent made of animal skins

**tie** one of many pieces of wood on which railroad tracks are laid

**toll** the price that someone must pay to use a road, bridge, or tunnel

**trader** a person who purchases things by exchanging one type of goods for another

**transcontinental railroad** train tracks going across a continent

**transportation** a means to move people and freight from one place to another

**trestle** a framework of wood or metal used as a bridge to support railroad tracks or a road

**wagon train** a group of covered wagons that traveled to the West together

# Timeline

**1730s** The first stagecoaches are used in the United States

**1785** Congress begins a mail service by stagecoach

**1787** John Fitch runs the first workable steamboat

**1807** Steamboats begin carrying passengers and freight in the United States

**1825** Workers complete the Erie Canal that connects the Great Lakes to the Atlantic Ocean

**1830** Peter Cooper's *Tom Thumb* locomotive races a horse-drawn wagon; *Best Friend of Charleston* starts America's first regular passenger train service

**1841** The first organized wagon trains head for Oregon and California

**1848** The gold rush begins in California

**1852** Wells, Fargo & Company begins its first bank and express stagecoach service in California

**1856** The first railroad bridge across the Mississippi River opens; the first recorded stagecoach robbery occurs

**1860** The Paiute War between Pauite Indians and white settlers delays the Pony Express service

**1860–1861** The Pony Express delivers mail to California from Missouri

**1861** The first telegraph message is sent across the continent

**1861–1865** The Civil War is fought between southern and northern states

**1862** President Lincoln signs the Pacific Railway Act to start building the transcontinental railroad; Congress passes the Homestead Act, giving land to settlers in the West

**1864** George Pullman builds a railroad sleeping car

**1869** The transcontinental railroad is completed

**1877** The Great Railroad Strike at the B&O Railroad begins in Martinsburg, West Virginia

**1903** *The Great Train Robbery*, the first western movie, opens

**1908** Henry Ford starts to sell the popular Model T car

**1916** The last recorded stagecoach robbery occurs

**1925** The first diesel electric locomotive runs in the United States

# Information

## WEBSITES

American Experience (PBS): Transcontinental Railroad
**www.pbs.org/wgbh/amex/tcrr/**

America on the Move (National Museum of American History)
**http://americanhistory.si.edu/onthemove/themes/story_48_1.html**

Central Pacific Railroad Photographic History Museum
**www.cprr.org**

Eyewitness to History: Traveling the Erie Canal, 1836
**www.eyewitnesstohistory.com/eriecanal.htm**

Wells Fargo Stagecoach History
**www.wellsfargohistory.com/stagecoach/stagecoach_history.htm**

## BOOKS TO READ

Hynson, Colin. *A History of Railroads: From Past to Present.* Milwaukee, WI: Gareth Stevens Publishing, 2006.

Krensky, Stephen. *Calamity Jane.* Minneapolis: Millbrook Press, 2007.

Naylor, Phyllis Reynolds. *Emily's Fortune.* New York: Delacorte Press, 2010.

Olson, Nathan. *The Building of the Transcontinental Railroad.* Graphic Library. Mankato, MN: Capstone Press, 2007.

O'Mara, Jack. *How Railroads Shaped America.* New York: PowerKids Press, 2009.

Ray, Kurt. *New Roads, Canals, and Railroads in Early 19th-Century America: The Transportation Revolution.* New York: Rosen Publishing Group, 2004.

Thompson, Gare. *Riding with the Mail: The Story of the Pony Express.* Washington, DC: National Geographic, 2007.

Zimmermann, Karl R. *Steamboats: The Story of Lakers, Ferries, and Majestic Paddle-Wheelers.* Honesdale, PA: Boyds Mills Press, 2007.

# Index